JOHN SMITH
and the Survival of Jamestown

by Cynthia Clampitt

PEARSON
Scott
Foresman

Editorial Offices: Glenview, Illinois • Parsippany, New Jersey • New York, New York

Sales Offices: Needham, Massachusetts • Duluth, Georgia • Glenview, Illinois
Coppell, Texas • Sacramento, California • Mesa, Arizona

Virginia's Difficult Start

In 1584 Sir Walter Raleigh, an English explorer and soldier, sent people to explore North America. They returned with reports of a beautiful land with friendly people and many natural resources. Raleigh claimed the land for England and named it Virginia, one of the nicknames of Queen Elizabeth, England's ruler at the time.

England needed more land. The cities were crowded, but because England is an island, there was nowhere for people to move. England also had few natural resources. The people of England had watched as Spain and Portugal established many **colonies**. Perhaps England needed colonies too.

Raleigh sent a group to Virginia to found a colony, but problems started to arise. Supplies were lost, and people ran out of food. The settlers returned to England after one year. Raleigh tried again in April 1587, sending 150 farmers, women, and children to Roanoke Island. There were serious problems, especially with disease, but homes were built and the colony was established. The first English child born in North America, Virginia Dare, was born in August.

A small group sailed to England to get supplies, but when they returned, there was no trace of the colony. Not a single person was ever found, and no one knows what happened. The settlement is still known as the "Lost Colony."

This old map shows the area called Virginia, claimed by England, and the area called Florida, claimed by Spain. Both areas were much larger than the states that have those names now.

Raleigh could not afford to send more ships. It was now clear that settling North America would cost more than any one person could afford. The task would be left to England's **entrepreneurs**, people who start businesses with the hope of making a profit. A group of entrepreneurs in London decided to invest in North America.

In 1606 King James I gave this group a **charter**, or official permission, to start a colony in Virginia. This group of entrepreneurs called themselves the Virginia Company of London. They sold **shares**, or part ownership of the company, to raise money. Successful business owners and wealthy people could buy shares with the hope that there would be a profit. The company then hired men to lead the expedition. By December 1606 three ships were ready to depart.

3

Captain John Smith had already experienced a lifetime of adventure before he went to Jamestown.

John Smith's Background

Among the men hired by the Virginia Company was Captain John Smith. Smith was the son of a farmer. He had some formal education, but much of his learning was the result of his love of reading. When both of his parents died, sixteen-year-old Smith decided to leave his quiet, humble life and head to the Netherlands to help the Dutch fight for freedom from Spain.

Smith returned to England for a while to study, but when invading Turks threatened Austria and Hungary, Smith went to help the Austrian army. However, the Turks triumphed, and Smith was captured and taken as an enslaved person to Turkey. Eventually, he escaped. By the time he returned to London after four years of being away, Smith was an expert on survival in foreign lands. This made him a natural choice for helping to settle Virginia.

The Powhatan

Algonquian is a family of languages spoken by North American Indian groups from Canada and the Great Lakes in the north, to the Rocky Mountains in the west, to North Carolina in the south. Many different groups of American Indians (also called Native Americans) are still described as Algonquian-speaking people.

Powhatan was the head of an Algonquian-speaking group that had migrated to Virginia during the 1500s. Powhatan's father had defeated the American Indian groups that had previously lived in the region. Powhatan continued to conquer the surrounding groups, forming them into a **confederacy** of at least thirty different Algonquian-speaking groups. The confederacy was named after the powerful chief who ruled them: the Powhatan. It is not known how much larger Powhatan's empire might have become if English colonists had not arrived.

Algonquian Words in English

Many Algonquian words were adopted into English because the words described things for which the new colonists had no names. Here are a few of the many words from Algonquian languages that you may recognize:

hickory	pecan	skunk
moose	powwow	toboggan
moccasin	raccoon	tomahawk

The Colonists Arrive

Because James I was King of England, both the new colony and the river near which it was built were named after him. The ships sent by the Virginia Company reached the site of what was to become Jamestown on May 14, 1607. The colonists had chosen a spot on the banks of the James River that was sixty miles from the mouth of Chesapeake Bay. They did not want to be too far from water, but they also wanted to be far enough inland to avoid cannon fire from any Spanish ships that might come from Florida.

All that the colonists had was what they brought with them on the ships, mostly tools, seeds, and some food. They had to create everything else they would need to survive—even building materials. Fortunately for the colonists, John Smith was a skilled survivor. He was soon directing the clearing of land and the building of houses. The colonists began to realize they needed his leadership.

As soon as the colonists landed, they began to unload the tools they would need to build the colony.

Because of continued attacks, the colonists built a wooden fort for protection.

Not long after they landed, the colonists were attacked by members of the Powhatan confederacy. Protection suddenly became a priority for Jamestown. There were only a few more than a hundred men and boys available to both work and stand guard, and many of them had no useful skills or were not used to hard work. However, in little more than a month, the colonists managed to build a wooden protective wall around the church, storehouse, and small group of houses they had constructed.

The next big concern was food. The colonists had brought farming tools, and they began to plant the seeds they had brought. However, in the marshy soil of Jamestown, they had difficulty growing English crops. John Smith, always interested in learning, went exploring to see if there were any local foods that might help them, as well as to study the surrounding region.

Even while being held prisoner, John Smith worked hard to get along with the American Indians and to learn from them.

Captain Smith Makes a Difference

As Smith was exploring in December 1607, he was surprised by an American Indian hunting party. The people with him were killed, and Smith was taken prisoner. The hunters presented Smith to Powhatan himself. Smith was very impressed with the "Great Emperor" Powhatan. Powhatan kept Smith as a prisoner for about four weeks, but Smith showed such courage—and such interest in Powhatan's people and culture—that Powhatan came to respect him.

One of the best-known stories from this time is about Pocahontas saving John Smith from being killed by Powhatan. This is what Smith truly believed happened. However, many historians now believe that the "killing" was part of a ceremony. After the ceremony, Powhatan called Smith his son, and Smith was no longer a prisoner.

Smith realized that the colonists' lives depended on their getting along with and learning from the American Indians. He learned the language and sent the sons of colonists to live with Powhatan families, so they would learn the language too. He thought it was important that Europeans know about American Indian culture. He wrote about American Indian laws, customs, and agriculture. The books he wrote are still among the most important sources of information on what these groups were like.

The colonists began to **barter** with the Powhatan people. Farming tools, pots, and other useful objects from England were traded for food, which kept the colonists alive. Smith wrote that it was Pocahontas who was most responsible for helping the colonists survive.

John Smith also realized that **cooperation** among the colonists was important. They had to work together—and they all had to work. Smith became famous for ordering that anyone who refused to work would not eat. This order angered some of the men who had come along. They felt that people like them should not work, but Smith made sure everyone did his fair share.

Who is Matoaka?

Powhatan's daughter was actually named Matoaka. "Pocahontas" was a nickname.

John Smith was successful at trading with the Powhatan people.

More colonists arrived in Jamestown in 1608. The colony continued to have problems, but in September 1608 Smith was elected president of Jamestown, and things began to improve. He had the fort expanded; he began training people in skills the colony needed. Twenty houses were built, crops were planted, and colonists began fishing regularly. It looked like Smith would make the colony a success.

Smith put the **needs** of the colony ahead of the **wants** of the Virginia Company. The company wanted him to search for gold, but Smith was busy keeping the colonists alive. Between the complaints of the men who did not want to work and the company's disappointment in Smith's failure to search for gold, the Virginia Company decided that Smith should be replaced. Smith worked hard to stay in Virginia, but in September 1609, he was badly burned by a gunpowder fire and was forced to return to England.

The Starving Time

The winter after John Smith left almost brought the end of Jamestown. Diseases had always been a big problem for the colonists, and many had died from malaria and other illnesses. Now they did not have Smith to get corn from the Powhatan. The winter of 1609–1610 became known as the Starving Time. By the end of the winter, only 60 people were left alive of the 214 who had been in Jamestown before the Starving Time.

The colonists were ready to give up. They buried their cannon and armor, and they abandoned the town. When an English ship arrived in May of 1610, the few surviving colonists decided to return to England. However, as the weak and ragged colonists sailed away from Virginia, they met another ship from England. They were told that more ships, supplies, and colonists were on the way. They turned back and returned to Jamestown.

The colonists who survived disease and starvation carried the dead out of the fort for burial.

Starting Over

Among the people on the ships that arrived in Jamestown was Lord De la Warr. The Virginia Company had given De la Warr more power than it had given John Smith. He could force the colonists to work and remove anyone on the council who tried to work against him.

De la Warr was not as wise in dealing with the Powhatan as he was with the English, however. He thought he should be tough with the American Indians, so he attacked some of the area's groups. Before long, the colonists were at war with the Powhatan.

The colony still continued to grow and more colonists arrived. Back in England, John Smith had written that North America offered opportunities, but it did not offer easy riches—people would have to work if they went to Virginia. Because of Smith's writings, the people now arriving were more willing to work hard. By 1613 there were more than seven hundred English colonists living in Virginia.

The biggest problem that still faced the colonists was how to make the colony profitable. The Virginia Company had watched Spanish ships return from South America loaded with gold. The Spanish had found new foods too, such as potatoes, chilies, chocolate, and tomatoes. The colony in Virginia had so far only produced hardship, death, and a few interesting books about plants and American Indians written by John Smith. What could the colony do?

Green Gold

It was John Rolfe who solved the money problem for the colony. He had traveled to the Caribbean before he went to Virginia. Rolfe he had gotten seeds from tobacco plants that the Spanish were growing in the Caribbean. Tobacco was discovered in the Americas, and it had become popular in Europe. He took these seeds with him when he sailed for Virginia in 1610. He felt that the land and climate in Virginia would be ideal for growing tobacco.

In 1613 Rolfe sent his first batch of tobacco to England, where it was a great success. Soon many other colonists began to plant tobacco. The demand for tobacco increased quickly. In 1616 the colonists shipped 2,500 pounds of tobacco to England, but in 1618 they shipped 20,000 pounds. Colonists even used tobacco to barter for goods.

Tobacco was the crop that finally made money for the Virginia colony.

Growing Pains in the Colony

Growing tobacco created problems too. The colonists were not growing as much food as they had before, because they were using so much land for tobacco. It takes a lot of work to grow tobacco, so hundreds of colonists were soon arriving in Virginia. As the Powhatan people tried to move farther away from the colonists, they found themselves getting closer to American Indian groups with whom they were enemies. The Powhatan began to strike back at the colonists, killing colonists or taking prisoners.

The English wanted the prisoners released, so they captured Pocahontas. They told Chief Powhatan that he could have his daughter back if he returned the English prisoners. While Pocahontas was with the English, she met John Rolfe. They fell in love, and in 1614 they were married. The marriage of Pocahontas and John Rolfe brought peace between the English and the Powhatan as long as Chief Powhatan lived.

King James Against Tobacco

While many people in England were eager to get tobacco, King James hated it. He wrote articles and passed laws trying to stop it from coming in. He wrote that it hurt people's health and smelled bad. He taxed merchants who sold tobacco, but even the king could not stop the increasing popularity of a plant that was making so much money for merchants.

Jamestown in the 1620s and 1630s was a growing town.

In 1619 the Virginia Company gave the colony some control over their government. The colonists elected their first representatives, called **burgesses**. When the burgesses met in July 1619, it was the first meeting of elected lawmakers in a European colony. It was the first time colonists had a voice in their government.

When Chief Powhatan died, his brother became the new chief. He wanted to get rid of the English. In 1622 he led an attack that killed 347 colonists. However, diseases killed hundreds more colonists than the attacks did.

In 1624 King James cancelled the charter he had given to the Virginia Company. There were too many problems for a group of entrepreneurs to solve. Virginia became a royal colony and Jamestown continued to grow. Jamestown was the capital of Virginia until 1699, when the government moved to Williamsburg.

Glossary

barter trading one kind of good or service for another without using money

burgess an elected representative

charter an official document giving a person or group permission to do something

colony a settlement of people who come from one country to live in another land

confederacy a union of groups, countries, or states that agrees to work together for a common goal

cooperation to work together to get things done

entrepreneur a person who starts a new business, hoping to make a profit

need something that a person must have in order to live

share part ownership in a company that gives each shareholder a say in how the business is run and a part of the profits

want something that a person would like to have but can live without